VOCABULARY
FOR THE
WORLD
OF
WORK
2
Everyday
Office & Business Words

by Donn Mosenfelder

EDUCATIONAL DESIGN, INC. EDI 327

ISBN# 0-87694-236-2   EDI 327

Table of Contents

1
JOB COMMUNICATION TERMS

Words in this chapter:

switchboard
extensions
hold button
intercom button
area code
person call
station call
collect call
charges are reversed
800 number
toll-free call
WATS line
incoming calls
outgoing calls
telegram
cable
night letter
teletypewriter
telex
metered mail
postage meter
mailing
bulk rate

sort
batch
zip code order
bag
bulk rate permit
indicia
first class
third class
parcel post
book rate
library rate
special delivery
registered
certified
return receipt requested
tracer
special handling
priority mail
express mail
addressee
return address
forwarding address
zip code

A Telephone Terms

The place where you get a job may have a **switchboard.** It may have many **extensions.** It may have phones with **hold buttons** and **intercom buttons.**

switchboard. A switchboard may have buttons you press to connect phone calls to different phones in the office. Or with the old switchboards, you plug in wires to connect to the different phones. The switchboard operator answers each call and puts it through to the right **extension** (see below).

extensions. Additional phones connected to the same phone line. Some people have extensions in their homes. In an office, each extension has its own extension number.

hold button. Some phones have a row of buttons. The first button may be a "hold" button. (The others are usually for different phone numbers or extensions, plus perhaps an **intercom** button — see below.) Let's say you have to stop talking to someone for the moment but you don't want to hang up. You press the hold button. Then when you're free, you can press the hold button again and can talk to the person once more. Pressing the hold button kept you from disconnecting the call. A hold button may be labeled with an H or the word HOLD.

intercom button. This is used to talk to someone in the office on a different extension. You press the intercom and dial that person's extension number. The other phone rings, and he or she presses the intercom to connect to you. Sometimes abbreviated **IC.**

Questions

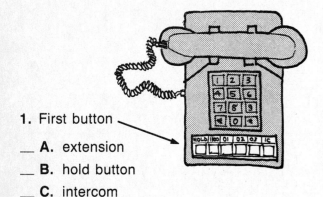

1. First button

__ **A.** extension

__ **B.** hold button

__ **C.** intercom

2. Last button.

__ **A.** extension

__ **B.** hold button

__ **C.** intercom

3. What kind of office would you expect might have a switchboard?

__ **A.** large office

__ **B.** office with only a few employees

4. What are extensions?

__ **A.** extra-long telephone wires

__ **B.** hold buttons and intercoms

__ **C.** several telephones, one telephone number

Most people on the job have to know how to use the telephone. This often means knowing how to make long distance calls.

Do you know about **area codes?** Do you know the difference between **person-to-person calls** and **station calls?**

    area code. The 3 extra numbers you have to dial when you make a long distance call. All of the numbers in an area have the same area code. On a long distance call you dial the area code before the regular number, and you may have to dial "1" before the area code.

    person call (or **person-to-person call**). When you want to talk to one particular person you can ask the operator to call person-to-person. You pay extra for the call. But you don't pay anything unless the operator is able to get the person you want.

    station call (or **station-to-station call**). This is the normal way of making a long distance call. It is much cheaper than a person-to-person call. But if someone answers, you pay for the call no matter who the person is.

Questions

1. Our number at work is (212) 255-7900. Which numbers are the area code?

— — —

2. Match.

__ You dial long distance. The charges start as soon as someone answers the phone.

__ You dial long distance. The operator asks for the person you want to talk to.

A. person call

B. station call

◆

Do you know what a **collect call** is, where the **charges are reversed?**

    collect call. If you don't want to pay for a call you can ask the operator to make the call "collect." If the person you are calling "accepts" the call, he or she will pay the charges.

    charges are reversed. This means that the call is collect.

Questions

1. Max calls Sarah collect. Who pays for the call?

   __ **A.** Max

   __ **B.** Sarah

2. Elaine calls Robert. The charges are reversed. Who pays for the call?

   __ **A.** Elaine

   __ **B.** Robert

Does the place where you work have an **800 number** for **toll-free calls?** Does it have a **WATS line** for **outgoing** calls?

> **800 number.** You can call some businesses long distance using their 800 numbers. The long distance number starts with 800 instead of a normal area code. When you use its 800 number to call a company, you don't pay anything. The company picks up the charge. The 800 number is only good for long distance calls. You can't use it to call locally.

> **toll-free call.** "Toll free" is another way of saying there is no charge — the call costs you nothing. An 800 number is a toll-free number.

> **WATS line.** Some companies have a WATS line to allow you to make long distance calls to certain parts of the country more cheaply. WATS stands for **W**ide **A**rea **T**elephone **S**ervice. One type of WATS is the type described here, for **outgoing** calls. Another type of WATS line is an 800 number, for **incoming** calls.

> **incoming call — outgoing calls.** Incoming calls are the calls made to you. Outgoing calls are the calls you make.

Questions

1. Donna works for a company that sells things by telephone. The people in her company can make calls anyplace in the country at a low cost per call.

   __ **A.** 800 number

   __ **B.** WATS line

2. Gino calls the Mellon Company on the Mellon Company's 800 line. Who pays for the call?

   __ **A.** Gino

   __ **B.** The Mellon Co.

3. Match.

   __ make a call   **A.** incoming

   __ receive a call   **B.** outgoing

4. Who pays the toll on a toll-free call?

   __ **A.** person who makes the call

   __ **B.** company receiving the call

   __ **C.** no one

B Telex Terms

The telephone is not the only way to send a message.

Another way is to send a *telegram* or a *cable.* To save money you might want to send a *night letter.*

telegram. A way of sending a message word for word to a distant place. You write out or phone in the message. Then the company that sends telegrams (usually Western Union) sends the message by means of electric wires ("cables") or radio waves. In a telegram you pay by number of words used. (In a long distance telephone call you pay according to the amount of time the call takes.)

cable. A telegram you send overseas is often called a cable.

night letter. A less expensive kind of telegram. It isn't delivered until the next morning (instead of being delivered right away).

Questions

1. You want to send a cable overseas. You don't care if it doesn't get there until the next day. What's the best way?

___ A. night letter
___ B. regular cable

2. What is the advantage of a night letter over a regular cable?

___ A. cheaper
___ B. faster

3. Match.

___ you send a word-for-word message

___ you talk to the other person

A. telegram
B. telephone

Some businesses have their own **teletypewriter** machines to send and receive **telexes.**

teletypewriter. A machine for sending **telex** messages (see below). You type out your message on it the way you type on a typewriter. Then it sends the message. A teletypewriter on the other end automatically prints the message you typed. Also called a **telex machine.**

telex. A telegram or cable you send by having a teletypewriter machine in your own office, which then communicates directly with a teletypewriter in the office you're contacting.

Questions

1. Match.

___ teletypewriter   **A.** machine

___ telegram   **B.** message

2. Telex.

___ **A.** short for telegram

___ **B.** short for telephone

Review

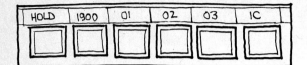

1. On your job you have a row of buttons on your phone, like the one above. Your phone rings. It's the type of ring you get when someone in the office on another extension wants to talk to you. Which button do you push when you pick up the phone?

    __ **A.** H
    __ **B.** 01
    __ **C.** IC

2. You are talking to someone on the 01 line. The 02 line starts ringing. To hold the 01 call while you answer 02, what button do you push?

    __ **A.** H
    __ **B.** 01
    __ **C.** IC

3. The local restaurant has a phone in the dining room and another phone in the kitchen, on the same number. What is the phone in the kitchen called?

    __ **A.** extension
    __ **B.** intercom
    __ **C.** switchboard

4. (206) 222-0336. Which numbers are the area code?

    __ __ __

5. A more expensive kind of long distance call. But you only pay if the operator connects you to the person you ask to talk to.

    __ **A.** person call
    __ **B.** station call

6. You call your brother collect. Who pays for the call?

    __ **A.** you
    __ **B.** your brother

7. Your company has both an 800 number and a WATS line for making calls anywhere in New England. Match.

    __ for incoming calls   **A.** 800 number
    __ for outgoing calls   **B.** WATS line

8. Your company has 2 telephone numbers: (201) 653-8766 and (800) 234-9377. Which number is a toll-free number for customers to use when they call you?

    __ **A.** (201) 653-8766
    __ **B.** (800) 234-9377

9. Which is cheaper?

    __ **A.** night letter
    __ **B.** regular telegram

10. What is a teletypewriter used for?

    __ **A.** to send or receive telexes
    __ **B.** to talk on the phone
    __ **C.** to type business letters

C Postal Terms

The place where you work is almost certain to send out a lot of mail — and to get a lot of mail.

If it is a big enough user of the mail, it will use **metered** mail. A **postage meter** can save a lot of time and effort.

metered mail. Instead of using stamps, metered mail is sent through a machine which puts the postage on. The amount of postage is stamped in red on the upper right-hand corner.

postage meter. The machine that puts postage on metered mail. The machine keeps track of how much postage is used. When it runs out of postage, the owner has to buy more from the Post Office. Some postage meters can automatically put on postage and seal the envelopes at a very fast rate. You line up the envelopes, and they zip through.

Questions

1. Metered mail.

__ **A.** you lick stamps and put them on

__ **B.** you send the mail through a machine

2. What are some of the possible advantages of postage meters? (Check one or more.)

__ **A.** fast

__ **B.** puts postage on

__ **C.** seals envelopes

__ **D.** types on addresses

Some firms do big *mailings.* They save money by sending out these mailings *bulk rate.* But they have to *sort* and *batch* the mail in *zip code order* and *bag* it. All this takes extra effort.

mailing. A large amount of mail going out at the same time to different people. In a typical big mailing, the same letter and/or printed matter goes to everyone. Big mailings are used for advertising and announcements.

bulk rate. A cheap way of sending large mailings (200 or more pieces that all contain the same letter or printed matter). The postage costs less, but the mailing has to be done in a certain way for the Post Office to allow the bulk rate.

sort. To put in order. Bulk rate mailings are sorted according to *zip code order* (see below).

zip code order. The zip code is the number at the end of an address. Mail sorted in zip code order is arranged in order from the lowest zip code to the highest.

batch. A group of 15-20 mailing pieces, arranged in zip code order and held together by paper bands or rubber bands. Also, to put mailing pieces in batches.

bag. To put batches of mail into large Post Office bags to be taken to the Post Office.

Questions

1. What is the advantage of sending out mail bulk rate?

__ **A.** cheaper

__ **B.** faster

2. You want to send letters to 3 of your friends. Can you send them out bulk rate?

__ yes   __ no

3. Our address is 47 W. 13 St., New York, N.Y. 10011. What is our zip code?

_____

4. Sort these 3 zip codes.

09402   73711   91415

_____ lowest

_____ middle

_____ highest

5. You're getting together a bulk rate mailing. You've put the pieces to be mailed in zip code order. You've put postage on. What's the next step?

__ **A.** batch and then bag

__ **B.** take to Post Office

You need a **bulk rate permit** (from the Post Office) to do bulk rate mailings. Some companies use *indicia* for these mailings.

> **bulk rate permit.** Allows a company to do bulk rate mailings. Each permit has a different number.

> **indicia.** Instead of using stamps or metering, the company may print on the envelope the special bulk rate number it has been assigned for bulk mailings. These printed markings for bulk mailings are called *indicia.*

Questions

1. Match.

__ printer puts it on   **A.** indicia

__ you put it through   **B.** metered
     postage machine

2. What is the purpose of a bulk rate permit?

__ **A.** lets you do big mailings cheaper

__ **B.** lets you use postage meter

Some mail is sent out *first class.* Other mail is sent out *third class.*

> **first class.** The usual way of sending letters. You are charged by the ounce.

> **third class.** If they weigh less than a pound, books, catalogs, and most packages can go out third class. If the package weighs more than a few ounces, third class is cheaper than first class. But it doesn't go through the mails as fast.

Question

1. Match.

__ letter to friend   **A.** first class

__ book weighing half a   **B.** third class
     pound

Most packages weighing more than 1 pound are mailed *parcel post.* Businesses can some-times save money on postage by sending out packages *book rate* or *library rate.*

parcel post. Class of mail for packages over 1 pound.

book rate. Inexpensive way of mailing books. It costs less than ordinary parcel post. But it's only for books.

library rate. Even cheaper than book rate. But it's only for books being mailed to libraries.

Questions

1. Match.

__ letter to friend

__ book weighing ½ pound

__ book weighing 2 pounds

A. first class

B. book rate

C. third class

2. Which is cheaper?

__ **A.** book rate

__ **B.** parcel post

3. One of our books to a library in Maine. Match.

__ book rate

__ library rate

__ parcel post

A. 35¢

B. 63¢

C. $1.61

◆

If you pay extra you can send out mail *special delivery.* You may want to send it *registered* or *certified,* and with *return receipt requested.*

special delivery. Special delivery mail is delivered by a special letter carrier instead of as part of the regular delivery. You pay extra for special delivery, but it should get there faster.

registered. This is for packages or valuables that you want to make sure get deli-vered to the right person. A registered package goes out insured. And the person who receives it also has to sign for it. Registered mail is more expensive than *cer-tified* mail (see below) — and safer.

certified. Like registered mail, but it's cheaper and not quite as safe. Certified mail is not insured, but the person receiving it still has to sign for it. If this person is not home when the mail arrives, the mail carrier will take the certified mail back to the Post Office and leave a message for the person to pick it up.

return receipt requested. The person who receives the package or piece of mail signs a *receipt* — a piece of paper that says he or she received it. This receipt is sent back to you after the item is delivered. You can keep it as a record. You can ask for a return receipt for either certified or registered mail, or for any other insured mail. But you pay extra.

Questions

1. Match.

___ the regular way   **A.** certified
___ signed for   or registered

                     B. first class

2. Insured.

___ **A.** certified
___ **B.** registered

3. What is the advantage of special delivery?

___ **A.** faster
___ **B.** gives you proof you sent it

4. You're sending a letter to your landlord. You don't have to insure it. You want a receipt to prove you sent it. How should the letter go out? (Check one or more.)

___ **A.** special delivery
___ **B.** registered
___ **C.** certified, return receipt requested

If you think insured mail is lost you can put a *tracer* on it.

     tracer. The Post Office checks to see if the insured package was delivered.

Questions

1. As used here, *tracer* means —

___ **A.** bullet
___ **B.** copy
___ **C.** search

2. You can only put a tracer on insured mail. Can you put a tracer on a special delivery letter?

___ yes   ___ no

You pay extra for **special handling** of packages. You pay even more for **priority mail.** The most expensive of all is **express mail.**

special handling. This is only for packages. The extra charge is to have the package moved out faster than regular Parcel Post (but not as fast as **priority mail** — see below). Special handling is a good way to send packages at Christmas time, when the mail is slow.

priority mail. Here you pay to have the package sent out in the same mail bag as first-class letters. Priority mail is usually faster than parcel post or special handling, for sending packages.

express mail. When you send out a package or letter express mail, the Post Office guarantees it will arrive in 24 hours ("overnight") to most locations, and within a few days to the other locations. Otherwise, you'll get your money back. Express mail is expensive, but very fast. (Note that there are also many **air express** companies, such as Federal Express and Purolator, which for a fee promise the same type of very rapid delivery of letters or packages.)

Questions

1. Put in order, slowest to fastest.

___ slowest   **A.** express

___ faster   **B.** priority

___ still faster   **C.** regular parcel post

___ fastest   **D.** special handling

2. Guaranteed delivery next day.

___ **A.** express

___ **B.** priority

___ **C.** special handling

3. Ways of mailing packages (check one or more).

___ **A.** first class

___ **B.** third class

___ **C.** priority

___ **D.** special handling

4. Do you remember the difference between third class and parcel post? Match.

___ under a pound   **A.** third class

___ more than a pound   **B.** parcel post

Do you know who the *addressee* is on an envelope?

Do you know where to put the *return address?*

Do you know what a *forwarding address* is?

Do you make sure to include a *zip code* when you write up an address?

addressee. Person or place you're writing to.

return address. Your name and address. The place where the mail should be returned if it can't be delivered. You put the return address on the upper left-hand corner of the envelope. Businesses usually use envelopes with their return address printed on them.

forwarding address. If you move, you give the Post Office your *forwarding address.* Mail sent to the old address will be delivered ("forwarded") to your new address.

zip code. You've seen this before. It's the number that goes at the end of an address. It is much easier for the Post Office to deliver mail when the zip code is included.

Questions

1. Match.

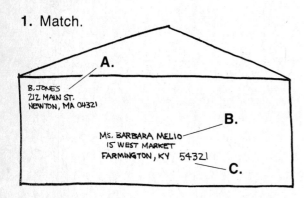

__ addressee

__ return address

__ zip code

2. Match.

__ mail sent back (couldn't be delivered)

__ you've moved

A. forwarding address

B. return address

Chapter Review

1. Anita's address is 375 Holly Drive, Smithville, Cal. 95303. What is her zip code?

_____

2. Anita is sending a letter to Boris. Who is the addressee?

__ **A.** Anita

__ **B.** Boris

3. Where does Anita put her own address on this envelope?

__ **A.**

__ **B.**

4. What is a forwarding address?

__ **A.** new address, when you move

__ **B.** return address

5. When would you use a tracer?

__ **A.** to make mail go faster

__ **B.** when you think a registered package got lost

6. Match.

__ postage put on by machine   **A.** indicia

__ printer prints it on   **B.** metered mail

7. Match.

__ cheap   **A.** bulk rate

__ faster   **B.** certified

__ signed for   **C.** special delivery

8. Match.

__ simple letter   **A.** first class

__ small package   **B.** parcel post

__ big package   **C.** third class

9. Match.

__ sort, batch, bag   **A.** bulk rate

__ insured package   **B.** registered

10. Match.

__ regular mail   **A.** express

__ faster   **B.** parcel post

__ 24 hours   **C.** priority

11. Match.

__ for long distance calls   **A.** area code

__ for mail   **B.** zip code

12. Match.

__ cheaper   **A.** person call

__ more expensive   **B.** station call

13. Match.

__ cheaper   **A.** night letter

__ faster   **B.** regular telegram

14. Match.

__ telex   **A.** cable

__ 800 number   **B.** toll-free number

15. Match.

__ button phone   **A.** for cheaper outgoing calls

__ WATS line

    B. has hold and intercom

2
GENERAL OFFICE VOCABULARY

Words in this chapter:

stapler

Rolodex

calculator

photocopy machine

Xerox

word processor

Selectric typewriter

service contract (or agreement)

maintenance contract

manila envelope

file folder

legal size pads

number 10 envelope

ledger sheets

files

alphabetical sorting

numerical sorting

account

indexing

collating

A Things in an Office

In most office jobs you use such things as **staplers, Rolodexes,** and **calculators.**

stapler. A device you push to bend a small piece of wire through sheets of paper to hold them together.

Rolodex. A device that holds little cards and can be moved around in a circular motion. You use Rolodexes to keep lists, for example a list of telephone numbers. When a number changes you pull out the old card and throw it away.

calculator. A device for doing arithmetic. The calculators you have probably seen the most are the small ones that fit in your hand. These are widely used in offices.

Question

1. Match.

__ for adding up numbers   **A.** calculator

__ for attaching sheets of   **B.** Rolodex
paper together

                         C. stapler

__ for names, addresses,
and phone numbers

◆

Offices have special machines. For example: **photocopy** machines, **word processors,** and **Selectric typewriters.**

photocopy machine. A machine that prints copies of letters, books, pages and so on. A **Xerox** is just one brand of copier, but people sometimes wrongly use the name "Xerox" for any photocopy machine. Modern photocopiers can copy not only printed matter but even pictures.

word processor. A computer device that is used in writing and typing. A word processor will "store" what you've typed on it. You can change a letter, a word, or a line at a time. You can also give it directions to tell it how to line things up, how big the type should be, and so on. When you are all finished you can have it type out automatically the finished letter or memo. And if you want you can have it type out several copies.

Selectric typewriter. A kind of typewriter, manufactured by IBM, that has its type on a metallic ball. Other manufacturers make similar machines.

Questions

1. Which would you think is more likely to have a large "memory"?

___ **A.** photocopy machine

___ **B.** word processor

2. You put the paper on top of the glass, close the cover, and push a button. The machine lights up, and a few seconds later a copy of the page comes out.

___ **A.** photocopier

___ **B.** Selectric

3. Selectric typewriter.

___ **A.** all the letters on a round globe

___ **B.** each letter on a separate metal arm

◆

The machines in an office sometimes break down. That is why offices often have **service contracts** (sometimes called **service agreements,** or **maintenance contracts**).

> **service contract.** Your company pays a set amount to a company that does repairs to keep a particular machine in working order. The contract is usually for a year at a time. Anytime the machine breaks down you call the service company. Someone comes and fixes the machine without any extra charge.

service agreement — maintenance contract. Same as **service contract.**

Questions

1. Service contract.

___ **A.** costs $65 per year per machine, no charge when you have to call for service

___ **B.** costs $20 per hour every time the service person comes to fix the machine

2. **Service agreement** and **maintenance contract** mean the same. Match the words that have about the same meaning.

___ service   **A.** maintenance

___ agreement   **B.** contract

◆

Offices often use special types of paper and supplies. For example: *manila envelopes, file folders, legal size pads, number 10 envelopes,* and *ledger sheets.*

manila envelope. An envelope made of a fairly strong brown paper. Large envelopes are often manila envelopes.

file folder. A folder to hold loose papers. File folders are usually made of a yellowish shiny cardboard. They are folded in the middle. A tab sticks out at the end. You put the name or number of the folder on the tab, and this is the name or number you use when you put the file in its place in the file drawer.

legal size pads. Extra-long pads of paper, often yellow in color. Most pads are 11 inches long. Legal pads are 14 inches.

number 10 envelopes. Regular envelopes, 9½ inches long and about 4 inches high, for business letters.

ledger sheets. Sheets of paper that have special lines printed on them for use in keeping money records.

Questions

1. Match.

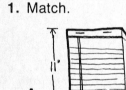 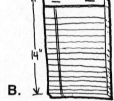

A.   B.

__ legal size pad
__ regular pad

2. Match.

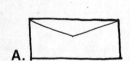 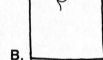

A.   B.

__ number 10 envelope
__ large manila envelope

3. Who do you think would be most likely to use ledger sheets?

__ **A.** bookkeeper
__ **B.** policeman
__ **C.** waiter

24

B Office Tasks

If you work in an office you will probably have to work with *files.* You may have to learn about *alphabetical sorting* and *numerical sorting* of *accounts.*

files. Metal drawers that hold records. The file cabinets in an office usually have 3, 4, or 5 drawers.

alphabetical sorting. Organizing a file according to the letters of the alphabet. (Names starting with "A" first, "B" second, and so on.)

numerical sorting. Organizing a file according to *account numbers* (see below).

account. Customers or suppliers your company deals with. Each account has a separate *account number.*

Questions

1. One of the file drawers in our office has all of the accounts from number 11001 to 14999.

    __ **A.** alphabetical sorting
    __ **B.** numerical sorting

2. Match.

    __ all names beginning with **A.** alphabetical
    "M"
    __ in order from 1 to 100   **B.** numerical

3. Our company sells books to the Woodstock Board of Education. Is the Woodstock Board of Education an account?

    __ yes   __ no

4. Our company buys paper from the North Star Paper Company. Is North Star Paper also one of our accounts?

    __ yes   __ no

5. What quality do you think is most important for working on the files in an office?

    __ **A.** good appearance
    __ **B.** careful
    __ **C.** strong

You may do *indexing* and *collating.*

> **indexing.** Putting a number or name on something, so it's ready for filing.

> **collating.** To put sheets of paper in order. In a typical collating job, let's say you've made 6 copies of each page of a memo with 5 pages. The copies of each page are all together. You have to separate them so that you wind up with 6 copies of the full memo, each one with the 5 pages in order.

Questions

1. One of the chapters in this book has 15 pages. When I finished writing it I made 3 copies of each page. The pages of each copy had to be put in order.

__ **A.** collate

__ **B.** index

2. One of the jobs in our office is to type up labels for each account folder.

__ **A.** collating

__ **B.** indexing

Chapter Review

1. Match.

__ add, subtract, multiply, and divide

__ for names and telephone numbers

__ puts sheets of paper together

__ type of computer

A. calculator

B. Rolodex

C. stapler

D. word processor

2. Match.

__ has bouncing ball

__ has metal drawers

__ Xerox machine

A. file cabinet

B. photocopy machine

C. Selectric

3. Match.

__ large brown envelope

__ regular envelope

A. manila envelope

B. number 10

4. Match.

__ 11 inches long

__ 14 inches long

A. legal size pad

B. regular pad

5. Match.

__ use to hold batch of papers

__ use to write up money records

A. file folder

B. ledger sheet

6. Match.

__ from 001 to 999

__ from A to D

A. alphabetical sorting

B. numerical sorting

7. Match.

__ put sheets of paper in order

__ put names on file folders

A. collate

B. index

8. Maintenance contract. (Check one or more.)

__ **A.** means same as service agreement

__ **B.** pay each time machine breaks down

__ **C.** pay for the whole year

9. Account, as used in this chapter.

__ **A.** customer or supplier

__ **B.** sales slip

__ **C.** story

3
BILLING TERMS

Words in this chapter:

purchase order	triplicate
P.O.	quadruplicate
P.O. number	allowance
requisition number	freight allowance
ASAP	prepaid
rush shipment	postpaid
F.O.B. point	C.O.D.
ship via	statement
ship-to address	overdue amount
bill-to address	accounts receivable (AR)
fulfill an order	customer service
invoice	credits
invoice number	returns
payment terms	credit memo
net 30	pro forma invoice
net 10	release the order
original copy	voucher
(bill in) duplicate	acknowledgement

A The Purchase Order

When a company orders goods it is likely to issue a **purchase order** (or **P.O.**).

The purchase order will show such things as the **P.O. number.** It will sometimes show a **requisition number.**

purchase order. A printed form which you fill out to tell what is being ordered and how it is to be shipped and billed.

P.O. Short for purchase order.

P.O. number. The company has a different number for each P.O. This makes it easier for the buyer and the seller to keep track of the P.O.

requisition number. Different from the P.O. number. In big companies you may have to fill out a requisition form asking (or "requesting" or **requisitioning**) that a P.O. be issued. The requisition is also a form, and each requisition has a different number. The requisition numbers and P.O. numbers are in different sequences.

Questions

1. Which comes first?

__ **A.** purchase order
__ **B.** requisition

2. What number does a requisition have?

__ **A.** same as P.O.
__ **B.** different from P.O.

3. "To requisition" means —

__ **A.** to ask
__ **B.** to order
__ **C.** to refuse

4. Our office manager just sent an order to Sweet's Office Supplies for 100 legal size pads. What form did she use?

__ **A.** P.O.
__ **B.** requisition

The P.O. will show both the date of the order and the date the goods are required. Customers often ask that their orders be shipped **ASAP.** Sometimes they specify the exact date on which they need the goods. Sometimes they ask for a **rush shipment.**

ASAP. Short for **as** **s**oon **as p**ossible.

rush shipment. A request for a **rush** is a request that the goods be shipped immediately — in a real hurry. A request for a **rush shipment** asks for faster shipment than ASAP.

Question

1. Match.

__ ship today or tomorrow   **A.** ASAP

__ OK if it's shipped in 2   **B.** rush
     weeks

The P.O. may show the **F.O.B. point.** It may tell how to **ship via.**

F.O.B. point. *F.O.B.* stands literally for "free **on** board." The **F.O.B. point** tells who pays the shipping. If it's "F.O.B. factory," the goods change hands at the factory, when they are loaded on a truck, and the customer pays the shipping. If it's "F.O.B. destination," the seller pays the shipping (but may add on the charge when it bills the buyer), and the goods officially change hands when they arrive at the buyer's warehouse. A tough concept to understand.

ship via. Tells how the customer wants the goods shipped — what trucking company to use, for example.

Questions

1. Sweet's Office Supplies paid for the delivery of our 100 legal-size pads. The pads did not officially belong to us until they arrived at our office.

__ **A.** F.O.B. Sweet's

__ **B.** F.O.B. our office

2. When she wrote up another P.O., our office manager filled in "our warehouse" in one place and "parcel post" in another. Match.

__ our warehouse   **A.** F.O.B.

__ parcel post   **B.** ship via

The **ship-to address** on a purchase order is often different from the **bill-to address.**

> **ship-to address.** Where the goods are to be sent.

> **bill-to address.** Where the bill, or **invoice** (see next unit), is to be sent. In a typical case, the goods are sent to the company's warehouse **(ship-to address),** while the invoice is sent to the business office **(bill-to address).**

Question

1. Lincoln High School orders many of our books for its reading department. The bills are paid by the Scott County Board of Education. Match.

    __ Lincoln High School   **A.** bill-to

    __ Scott County Board of   **B.** ship-to
    Education

Review

1. Match.

    __ tells what trucker to use   **A.** F.O.B. point

    __ tells who pays the trucker   **B.** ship via

2. Match.

    __ ask   **A.** P.O.

    __ order   **B.** requisition

3. Match.

    __ gets the goods   **A.** bill-to

    __ pays for them   **B.** ship-to

4. Which calls for faster shipment?

    __ **A.** ASAP

    __ **B.** rush

B The Invoice

As you know, the customer often issues a P.O. The selling company **fulfills the order** and issues an **invoice.**

> **fulfill an order.** To ship and bill an order.

> **invoice.** A bill. Tells what the buyer bought and how much it cost. The buyer may get the invoice when the goods arrive. Or the invoice may be sent out separately.

Questions

1. Fulfill, as used here.

__ **A.** complete

__ **B.** feel good

2. Match.

__ invoice

__ P.O.

A. what you want

B. what you owe for it

◆

Each invoice has an **invoice number.** Like the P.O., the invoice will show ship-to and bill-to addresses. It will show the P.O. number, the F.O.B. point, and the date of the order. Most invoices also show **payment terms.**

> **invoice number.** The selling company assigns a different number to each invoice.

> **payment terms.** When you're supposed to pay. For example, whether you are supposed to pay immediately, or perhaps after a certain amount of time. Also called just **terms** for short.

Questions

1. Match.

__ when someone asks that goods be ordered

__ when the order is written up

__ when the order is shipped

A. invoice number

B. P.O. number

C. requisition number

2. As used here, **terms** refers to —

__ **A.** letters

__ **B.** names

__ **C.** time

◆

Typical terms are *net 30* or *net 10.*

> **net 30.** Means the bill is expected to be paid within 30 days of the time the goods were received.

> **net 10.** Means the bill is expected to be paid within 10 days.

Question

1. The numbers in *net 30* and *net 10* refer to —

_ **A.** days

_ **B.** dollars

_ **C.** people

◆

The customer may simply receive the *original copy* of the invoice. Some customers ask to be billed in *duplicate* or *triplicate* (or even *quadruplicate*).

> **original copy.** The top copy. An invoice usually has a top copy, which you write on or type on, plus several carbon copies. The top copy goes to the customer.

> **duplicate.** When the customer is billed in duplicate it gets 2 copies of the invoice (the original plus one more).

> **triplicate.** The original invoice plus 2 other copies — 3 copies total.

> **quadruplicate.** The original plus 3 other copies — 4 copies total.

Questions

1. The ABC Co. needs copies of invoices for the bookkeeper, the main office, and the department that placed the order. It asks to be billed —

_ **A.** in duplicate

_ **B.** in triplicate

_ **C.** in quadruplicate

2. Match.

_ original   **A.** carbon copy

_ second copy   **B.** top copy

◆

34

The invoice may list any *allowances,* such as *freight allowances.*

allowance. An amount to be taken off the total owed. This could be a set amount, or a percent of the bill. As an example, a store might be given an allowance by the manufacturer to help pay for an ad to help sell the goods. Another type of allowance is a *freight allowance* (see below).

freight allowance. If there is a freight allowance, the buyer may have to pay the actual shipping charge. But as part of the deal the buyer gets a certain *allowance* for shipping. This allowance is an amount of money that is subtracted from the total amount on the invoice.

Questions

1. Freight allowance.

__ **A.** money

__ **B.** passengers

__ **C.** weight

2. Let's say the seller gives the buyer an allowance for advertising. This amount is —

__ **A.** added to the bill

__ **B.** subtracted from the bill

◆

Some orders are sent out with the shipping *prepaid,* or *postpaid.* Other orders are send out *C.O.D.*

prepaid. Paid in advance. If the shipping is prepaid, the seller pays it. Then the seller may or may not add the charges to the bill. (This depends on the "shipping terms" of the sale.)

postpaid. Means exactly the same as prepaid. They sound different, but they mean the same.

C.O.D. Short for **c**ollect **o**n **d**elivery. If *shipping* is C.O.D., the buyer pays the shipping charges when it receives the goods.
In some cases, the *whole order* — not just shipping, but the cost of the goods, too — is sent out C.O.D. Then the buyer pays the whole invoice amount when the goods arrive. The buyer pays the trucker, who then pays the sender of the goods.

Questions

1. In the words *prepaid* and *postpaid* —

__ **A.** "pre-" equals "post-"
__ **B.** "pre-" and "post-" are opposites

2. Smith & Co. buys plastic from J. P. Plastics. Shipping is prepaid. Who pays the trucker?

__ **A.** Smith & Co.
__ **B.** J. P. Plastics

3. Ralph Hines buys a desk from Royal Stores. Shipping on the desk is C.O.D. Who pays?

__ **A.** Ralph Hines
__ **B.** Royal Stores

Review

1. To bill in duplicate means to send _____ (how many?) copies.

2. Terms of net 10 means payment can be made in 10 _____.

3. *Prepaid* and *postpaid* mean —

__ **A.** the same
__ **B.** opposite

4. A bill is the same as —

__ **A.** an invoice
__ **B.** a P.O.

5. An order is sent out with shipping C.O.D. Who pays the trucker?

__ **A.** buyer
__ **B.** seller

6. To fulfill an order.

__ **A.** get it
__ **B.** ship it

7. Match.

__ allowance   **A.** money
__ payment terms   **B.** time

C Other Billing Terms

At the end of the month, if you still owe the company money, it will probably send you a **statement** showing the **overdue amount.**

> **statement.** Usually sent out monthly. Shows what you bought during the month, how much you paid, and how much you still owe. It will list any **overdue amounts** (see below).

> **overdue amount.** Amount that should have been paid already but is still owed.

Questions

1. Ralph Hines' desk was shipped on April 7. On May 1, Royal Stores sent out a reminder that Ralph still owed $230. Match.

   __ April 7   **A.** invoice
   __ May 1   **B.** statement

2. Ralph was supposed to have paid for the desk within 10 days of shipment. Was the $230 an overdue amount?

   __ yes   __ no

◆

Each order that is sent out becomes a part of **accounts receivable** (**AR,** for short).

Lost orders, late orders, and the like require **customer service.**

> **accounts receivable (AR).** Record of what goods the customers bought and how much money they owe the company. Many companies have a separate **accounts receivable department.** It does the billing and sends out statements.

> **customer service.** Handling customer complaints and problems.

Questions

1. Match.

___ customer   **A.** account

___ money owed   **B.** receivable

2. If you ordered one particular color of floor tiles and were sent another color, would this be a matter for customer service?

___ yes   ___ no

To take care of **credits** and **returns,** the seller issues **credit memos.**

credits. A "credit" on an invoice reduces the amount you owe. You might get a credit, for example, if one of the items you ordered arrived broken.

returns. You may have the right to return part of all of the things you bought. You get a credit for such returns.

credit memo. Like an invoice, except that it shows how much of a credit is being given against the amount owed. A credit memo shows that the seller owes **you** money, instead of the other way around.

Questions

1. **Returns,** as used here.

___ **A.** goods you sent back

___ **B.** how much money you made

___ **C.** who won the election

2. **Credit,** as used here.

___ **A.** borrow more money

___ **B.** pay money

___ **C.** subtract from the money you owe

3. Match.

___ buyer owes   **A.** credit memo

___ seller owes   **B.** invoice

Some customers may ask for *pro forma invoices.* This is often the case with customers from other countries.

Other customers may ask the seller to fill out a *voucher* (or *acknowledgement*).

pro forma invoice. An invoice sent in advance. It's exactly like the final invoice, but you sent it without actually shipping the goods. The customer who requests it needs it because of some special paperwork that has to be done before the order can be *released* (see below).

release the order. Give the go-ahead to ship.

voucher. A form the customer supplies which the seller is supposed to fill out, along with the invoice. It gives the same information as the invoice. The seller signs it as proof that the information on the voucher is correct. A customer who asks the seller to fill out a voucher needs it as part of the paperwork in paying for the purchase.

acknowledgement. Same as voucher.

Questions

1. Release the order.

__ **A.** cancel it

__ **B.** ship it

2. A customer in Japan asks us for a pro forma invoice on 10 of our programs. When do we ship the programs?

__ **A.** before we send the invoice

__ **B.** at the same time we send the invoice

__ **C.** when the customer tells us

3. A customer sends us a purchase order with a voucher. Match.

__ purchase order   **A.** fill it out, sign it, and return it

__ voucher

                                B. keep it for our files

4. *Acknowledgement,* as used here.

__ **A.** admit you lied

__ **B.** form you fill out

__ **C.** when you greet someone

Chapter Review

1. Match.

___ 1   **A.** duplicate

___ 2   **B.** original

___ 3   **C.** quadruplicate

___ 4   **D.** triplicate

2. Match.

___ **10**, in net 10   **A.** days

___ **allowance,** in   **B.** money
freight allowance

3. Match.

___ monthly   **A.** invoice

___ when the order is **B.** statement
shipped

4. Match.

___ buyer pays   **A.** C.O.D.

___ seller pays   **B.** prepaid

5. Match.

___ prepared by   **A.** invoice
buyer   **B.** purchase order

___ prepared by seller

6. Match.

___ AR   **A.** money owed

___ F.O.B.   **B.** order for goods

___ P.O.   **C.** where goods
change hands

7. Match.

___ goods sent back **A.** allowance

___ money off the bill **B.** return

8. Match.

___ late payment   **A.** customer service
problem
___ late shipment

                    B. overdue amount

9. Match.

___ F.O.B.   **A.** place

___ ship via   **B.** trucker

10. Match.

___ fast   **A.** ASAP

___ faster   **B.** rush

11. Match.

___ ask   **A.** release

___ OK   **B.** requisition

12. Match.

___ ship   **A.** credit

___ subtract money **B.** fulfill

13. Match.

___ shows seller   **A.** acknowledgement
owes money
                   B. credit memo
___ voucher

14. Pro forma invoice.

___ **A.** bill, don't ship

___ **B.** ship, don't bill

4
SHIPPING AND RECEIVING TERMS

Words in this chapter:

shipping label
packing list
bill of lading
waybill
pro number
receiving report
RR
partial shipment
short shipment
inventory
in stock
perpetual inventory
spot check

take inventory
physical count
parcel post
UPS
UPS Blue Label
freight
container
product shipper
corrugated
individual shipper
master carton
12-shipper

◆

A Paperwork in a Warehouse

The people who ship goods from a warehouse have plenty of paperwork, just like the people who do billing. First of all, each package has to have a **shipping label.** Inside, there is usually a **packing list.**

> **shipping label.** Label that gives the address of the customer.

> **packing list.** List of the products inside the package.

Question

1. Match.

___ packing list

___ shipping label

A. tells what you shipped

B. tells where to ship

---◆---

For truck shipments, a **bill of lading** is prepared. The trucking firm will prepare its own **waybill** and assign a **pro number.**

> **bill of lading.** A receipt for the goods which the truck driver signs. The seller prepares the bill of lading. It has a top copy and several carbons. It lists how many cartons are in the shipment, what they weigh, their destination, and so on. The truck driver signs the bill of lading. He or she gives one copy to the warehouse people and keeps the other copies for the records of the trucking company and the receiver of the goods.

> **waybill.** The bill, or invoice, the trucking company sends to whoever is paying for the shipment.

> **pro number.** The number the trucking company assigns to the shipment.

Questions

1. Match.

__ seller prepares, trucker signs   **A.** bill of lading

__ trucker prepares, seller pays   **B.** waybill

2. Where would you expect to find the pro number of a shipment?

__ **A.** on the bill of lading

__ **B.** on the waybill

When a shipment of goods arrives at the warehouse, a **receiving report** (or **RR**) is made. The person doing this has to be careful. There may be only a **partial shipment** or a **short shipment.**

> **receiving report.** Tells what was received: how many cartons, how many items in each carton, and so on.
>
> **RR.** Short for receiving report.
>
> **partial shipment.** A shipment of only part of the goods ordered.
>
> **short shipment.** A shipment that contains less than was promised.

Questions

1. Match.

__ AR   **A.** goods received

__ RR   **B.** money owed

2. Short shipment.

__ **A.** doesn't go very far

__ **B.** something missing

3. Partial shipment.

__ **A.** ordered 10, got 5

__ **B.** ordered 10, got 20

When goods come into the warehouse they are put into *inventory*. The people who keep track of goods *in stock* may keep a *perpetual inventory*. From time to time they will still do *spot checks*.

inventory. A list of all the goods on hand.

in stock. On hand, in inventory.

perpetual inventory. To keep a perpetual inventory, you keep a list of each kind of item in stock. You subtract from your counts every time you ship out something and add every time you receive something. This way, you always know exactly what you have in stock without re-counting everything all the time.

spot check. A spot check is an actual count of an item here or there, to see whether your perpetual inventory is correct. When you spot check you only count one thing or a few things at a time.

Questions

1. Inventory.

__ **A.** money

__ **B.** goods

2. Stock.

__ **A.** inventory

__ **B.** people

3. Spot check.

__ **A.** check for spots

__ **B.** check perpetual

4. You receive a truck full of goods. Does that change your perpetual inventory?

__ yes   __ no

5. Match.

__ actual count of items

__ add and subtract as goods come and go

A. perpetual inventory

B. spot checks

At least once a year, the people in the warehouse will **take inventory,** with **physical counts** on everything.

> **take inventory.** Count everything in stock. When you take inventory you count each carton. If they are all the same you open at least one up and count the things inside, sometimes by weighing them. And so on. When you finish taking the full inventory you know what you really have in stock. Then you can correct your perpetual inventory, which will probably be wrong here and there. Something may have been lost or stolen. Or you may have simply made an occasional mistake in the perpetual.

> **physical count.** An actual count, the type of count you do when you take inventory.

Questions

1. Match.

__ count stacks of boxes

__ keep track year round

A. perpetual inventory

B. physical count

2. Match.

__ count stock on hand

__ keeps books on stock on hand

A. perpetual inventory

B. take inventory

B Ways to Ship

Packages can be sent out *parcel post.* Or they can be sent out *UPS.* For speedy delivery they can be sent *UPS Blue Label.*

parcel post. You've seen this term before. Parcel post is a way of sending packages in the U.S. Mail.

UPS. Stands for **U**nited **P**arcel **S**ervice. UPS is a company that picks up and delivers packages. It is commonly used all over the United States. Many companies have UPS make regular pick-ups and deliveries every day.

UPS Blue Label. Fast way of shipping UPS. UPS Blue Label costs more, as you might imagine.

Questions

1. Through the mail.

__ **A.** parcel post

__ **B.** UPS

2. Match.

__ cheaper   **A.** regular UPS

__ faster   **B.** UPS Blue Label

Bigger *freight* shipments are usually sent out by truck. If the shipment is large enough it may fill up a whole *container.*

freight. Goods being shipped.

container. In trucking, a container is the back part of the truck, the trailer van, the big boxlike part of the truck that carries the goods. One standard size of container is 20 feet long. Another, larger size is 40 feet long.

Questions

1. Truck container.

__ **A.**

__ **B.**

2. You receive a full container of goods.

__ **A.** one box

__ **B.** many boxes

3. Freight.

__ **A.** goods in truck

__ **B.** goods in warehouse

Review

1. Match.

___ invoice   **A.** bill of lading

___ receipt   **B.** waybill

2. Who assigns the pro number?

___ **A.** seller

___ **B.** trucker

3. When do you make a receiving report?

___ **A.** when goods come in

___ **B.** when you take inventory

4. Which requires a physical count?

___ **A.** perpetual

___ **B.** spot check

5. In stock.

___ **A.** on hand

___ **B.** on the way

C Shipping Cartons

The *shippers* for products are often made of *corrugated.*

> **(product) shipper.** The outside box you put your product in to get it ready for shipment. The shipper should be strong enough so the goods won't get damaged in shipment.

> **corrugated.** The cardboard material used for most shipping cartons. It's usually brown. If you look at an edge carefully you'll see that there is brown paper on either side while inside there is a layer of wavy ridges. This makes the corrugated strong.

Questions

1. If you look at corrugated from the side, what do you see?

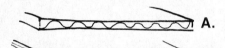

A.

B.

__ A.
__ B.

2. Product shipper.

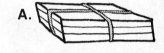

A.

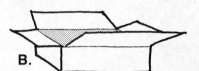

B.

__ A.
__ B.

Some goods are put in ***individual shippers.*** Others are put in ***master cartons***. A ***12-shipper*** is a typical master carton.

individual shipper. Holds only one of the items.

master carton. Holds several cartons. You sometimes put each item in its own carton and then put several of these cartons in a master carton.

12-shipper. A master carton that holds 12 individual cartons. A 6-shipper would hold 6 cartons; a 24-shipper would hold 24 cartons.

Questions

1. Match.

__ individual shipper

__ master carton

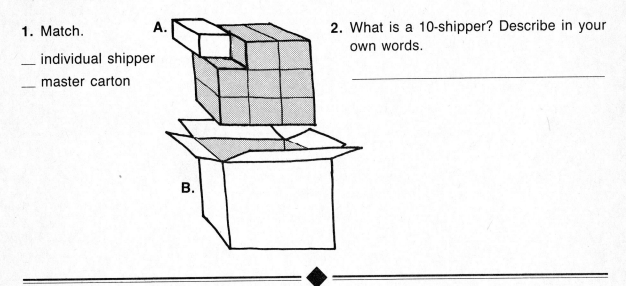

A.

B.

2. What is a 10-shipper? Describe in your own words.

_____

_____

Chapter Review

1. Product shipper.

___ **A.** the inside box
___ **B.** the outside box

2. What is the advantage of corrugated?

___ **A.** beautiful
___ **B.** strong

3. 12-shipper.

___ **A.** 12 feet long
___ **B.** costs $12
— **C.** holds 12 boxes

4. Match.

___ container
___ master carton

A. back of truck
B. made of corrugated

5. Match.

___ gives address
___ tells how many cartons

A. packing list
B. shipping label

6. Match.

___ seller prepares
___ trucker prepares

A. bill of lading
B. waybill

7. Match.

___ pro number
___ RR

A. trucker assigns
B. warehouse prepares

8. Match.

___ physical count
___ year around record

A. perpetual inventory
B. take inventory

9. Match.

___ goods being shipped
___ stock on hand

A. freight
B. inventory

10. Match.

___ send packages by mail
___ use Blue Label for fast shipment

A. parcel post
B. UPS

11. Individual shipper.

___ **A.** corrugated carton
___ **B.** trucker

12. Do you do a physical count when you spot check your inventory?

___ yes   ___ no

5
MARKETING AND SALES VOCABULARY

Words in this chapter:

marketing department
sales department
merchandising
product line
the trade
trade show
trade journal
trade association
promotion
promo
deal

demo
discount
markup
allowance
dating
closeout
discontinued item
overstocked item
overstock — out of stock
loss leader
premium

A General Terms

Marketing and sales are very close together. But a big company is likely to have both a *marketing department* and a *sales department*.

marketing department. The marketing department will plan which products will be sold, where they will be sold, and how they will be presented.

sales department. It will manage the sales force. The marketing people do the planning. The sales people do the actual selling.

Questions

1. Marketing department.

__ **A.** helps buy products

__ **B.** helps sell products

2. Match.

__ presents products to customers

__ decides on such things as prices and advertising

A. marketing

B. sales

Merchandising is an important part of marketing. Each product or *line of products* will be "merchandised" differently.

merchandising. Deciding how a product will look, how it will be advertised, how it will be displayed in stores, whether there will be any special offers made, and so on.

product line. A group of products that are similar or related. A big company may have several product lines. It may even have a separate sales force for each line.

Questions

1. To merchandise a product.

__ **A.** to make it more attractive to buyers

__ **B.** to manufacture it

__ **C.** to store it in the warehouse

2. *Line,* as in "line of products."

__ **A.** products put in a row

__ **B.** several similar products

People in a particular type of business sometimes talk of *"the trade."* And of course, each type of business may have its own *trade shows, trade journals,* and *trade associations.*

the trade. The companies that specialize in a certain type of business. For example, a toy company is part of the toy trade.

trade show. A show where companies in a particular type of business present their goods. Trade shows are usually just for people in the trade. In a toy show, for example, a manufacturer of toys will try to sell its toys to a buyer from a toy store. The manufacturers, importers, and distributors which present their toys at the toy show do *not* try to sell to the public.

trade journal. A magazine that specializes in news about a particular type of business.

trade association. An organization that is set up to help companies which specialize in a particular type of business. The toy industry has a toy manufacturers' association, for example. To receive the benefits of the association, you have to join it and pay dues.

Questions

1. Some companies only sell "to the trade." This means they only sell —

__ **A.** to the general public

__ **B.** to other companies

2. What happens in an electronics trade show?

__ **A.** customers can trade in their old radios and TVs

__ **B.** electronics manufacturers sell their products to electronics stores

3. Trade journal.

__ **A.** hand written

__ **B.** printed

4. Members of a trade association.

__ **A.** have to be good at trading

__ **B.** have to have the right kind of business

Review

1. Merchandising is a part of marketing.

__ true   __ false

2. Match.

__ trade association **A.** group
__ trade journal   **B.** magazine

3. A trade show is primarily for —

__ **A.** the general public
__ **B.** manufacturers, stores, and other businesses

4. Product line.

__ **A.** several copies of a product
__ **B.** several similar products

B Special Selling Terms

To market a particular product you may want to do a special **promotion,** or **promo.** You may put together a special **deal.**

> **promotion.** A special plan for advertising a product and presenting it. A promotion will often include a special offer — "Buy one, get the second free," for example — or a reduction in price — or some other special offer.

> **promo.** Short for promotion.

> **deal.** Special offer.

Questions

1. Who is more likely to plan a promotion?

_ **A.** marketing department
_ **B.** sales department

2. **Deal,** as used here.

_ **A.** in cards
_ **B.** in selling

3. Promo.

_ **A.** help in selling
_ **B.** new job
_ **C.** school dance

◆

A salesperson who presents an item is expected to be able to make a good **demo.**

> **demo.** Short for demonstration. When you **make a demo** you show how a product works — and why someone should buy it.

Question

1. Match.

_ demo   **A.** marketing
_ promo   **B.** sales

◆

Let's say you're selling an item wholesale to the trade. The customer wants to know what kind of **discount** you're offering and what kind of **markup** his or her company will have.

> **discount.** Amount of money subtracted from a cost or price. Your discount may be a percent. Let's say an item sells for $1 in stores. You offer it at a 40% discount. That is, you offer 40 cents off this price so that the store pays 60 cents.

> **markup.** An increase in price. In the example above, the store bought the item for 60 cents. It will charge its retail customers $1. Its markup is 40 cents.

Questions

1. You buy an item for $1.00. You mark it up 90¢. What do you sell it for?

$__.____

2. 50 percent discount.

__ **A.** ½ the price

__ **B.** twice the price

◆

Let's say you are selling your products wholesale. The deal you offer may have some **allowances.** You may offer **dating.**

> **allowance.** You've seen this term before. An allowance is a special price reduction. You may offer an **advertising allowance,** for example, to help stores pay for advertising your products. Or you may offer a **freight allowance,** to help customers pay for the shipping from your warehouse to their stores.

> **dating.** Delay in when the purchase has to be paid for. You may offer a deal where the customer doesn't have to pay for the purchase until 90 days after it receives the goods.

Question

1. Match.

__ allowance   **A.** money off

__ dating   **B.** payment terms

◆

You may offer special price reductions on a **closeout** or on **discontinued** or **overstocked items.**

> **closeout.** An item you are closing out. That is, an item you are going to stop making. You want to get rid of what you have on hand so you offer it cheaper.

> **discontinued items.** Same as closeout.

> **overstocked items.** Items you have too many of. You want to reduce your stock so you may offer them cheaper.

Questions

1. Discontinue.

___ **A.** go

___ **B.** stop

2. A manufacturer has been selling a particular item for $90. It decides to sell it as a closeout. What price will to probably charge?

___ **A.** less than $90

___ **B.** $90

___ **C.** more than $90

"Overstock" should not be confused with *out of stock.*

out of stock. You don't have any on hand. When you are overstocked you have too many. When you are out of stock, you don't have any.

Question

1. Match.

___ out of stock   **A.** lots

___ overstock   **B.** none

To get you to shop in a particular store, the store may offer a *loss leader.* Or it may offer a *premium.*

loss leader. A product offered for sale at a price *less* than the store paid for it.

premium. An item offered free, or at a very low price, as part of a deal. For example, you buy one item and you get a second item free, as a premium.

Questions

1. A store buys a type of soap for $1 per box. It decides to offer it to customers as a loss leader. What will it charge?

___ **A.** less than $1

___ **B.** $2 or more

2. You buy one pint of ice cream at full price and you can buy the second for just a penny. Which is the premium?

___ **A.** first pint

___ **B.** second pint

Chapter Review

1. Match.

___ marketing plan for a product   **A.** demo

___ sales presentation   **B.** promo

2. Match.

___ discount   **A.** add to price

___ markup   **B.** subtract from price

3. Match.

___ discontinued   **A.** closeout

___ out of stock   **B.** none

___ overstock   **C.** too many

4. Match.

___ loss leader   **A.** buy one, get second free

___ premium   **B.** sold below cost

5. Match.

___ dating   **A.** extra time to pay

___ deal   **B.** special offer

6. Match.

___ the line   **A.** businesses

___ the trade   **B.** products

7. Match.

___ demonstration   **A.** part of marketing

___ merchandising   **B.** part of sales

8. What do trade show, trade journal, and trade association have in common?

___ **A.** for businesses of a certain type

___ **B.** you can trade one for the other

6
BASIC COMPUTER VOCABULARY

Words in this chapter:

microcomputer
minicomputer
mainframe
keyboard
monitor
CRT
printer
computer terminal
computer hardware
computer software
computer disk
disk drive
hard disk

floppy disk
input
output
data entry
information retrieval
data processing
word processing
memory
program
computer programmer
computer language
BASIC
COBOL

A The Computer Itself

More and more businesses have computers. There will probably be a computer in the place where you work.

Some businesses use **microcomputers.** Most businesses use **minicomputers.** Very large businesses sometimes use a **mainframe computer.**

microcomputer. A personal computer, the type that is also found in homes and classrooms. A microcomputer can fit on a desk top.

minicomputer. A more powerful computer, with more uses. Some minicomputers are as large as an icebox.

mainframe computer. A very large computer. Can fill a whole room, or even several rooms.

Questions

1. Match.

___ micro

___ mini

A. small

B. smaller

2. Mainframe.

___ **A.** smaller than microcomputers and minicomputers

___ **B.** Larger than microcomputers and minicomputers

3. Most businesses use—

___ **A.** the smallest size computers

___ **B.** middle sized computers

___ **C.** the largest computers

A computer will have a *keyboard* and a *monitor,* and in businesses usually a *printer.*

keyboard. Like a typewriter. You type on it to "talk" to the computer.

monitor. A screen, like a TV screen. It shows you what you've typed and gives you instructions. Also called a *CRT* (for **C**athode **R**ay **T**ube, a tube like your TV tube).

printer. Types out the finished work of the computer.

terminal. A computer setup that consists of a keyboard and a monitor above. It's not a computer by itself, but several terminals may be connected to a big computer.

Questions

1. Match.

__ use your eyes   **A.** keyboard

__ use your fingers   **B.** monitor

2. Match.

__ used for showing com-   **A.** CRT
puter information on a
screen   **B.** printer

__ used for typing letters,
reports, and so on

3. Computer terminal.

__ **A.** needs a computer to work

__ **B.** works by itself

Have you heard people talk about *computer hardware* and *computer software*? Do you know what these terms mean?

computer hardware. The machines in a computer setup.

computer software. The "programs" that tell a computer what to do.

Questions

1. Match.

__ instructions to a computer

__ the computer itself

    A. hardware

    B. software

2. Keyboards, monitors, and printers.

__ **A.** computer hardware

__ **B.** computer software

Most business computers use *computer disks* and have some form of *disk drive*. One type of disk drive is for *hard disks*; another, for *floppy disks*.

computer disk. A plastic disk somewhat like a phonograph record. The disk stores computer information or computer programs.

disk drive. A computer with a disk drive works something like a record player. You put the disk in, and the disk drive feeds the information into the computer.

hard disk. Hard disks are like thick records inside plastic cases. Hard disks can store a lot of information, but they are very expensive.

floppy disk. Floppy disks look like thin, flexible records inside a square envelope. They can't store as much information as a hard disk, but they cost only a few dollars.

Questions

1. Computer disk.

__ **A.** round

__ **B.** square

2. Disk drive.

__ **A.** hardware

__ **B.** software

3. Match.

__ floppy disk

__ hard disk

    A. costs less than $10

    B. costs hundreds or thousands of dollars

Review

1. Most common computer in businesses.

__ A. mainframe
__ B. microcomputer
__ C. minicomputer

2. Match.

__ can fill a whole room   A. mainframe
__ personal computer   B. micro-
__ keyboard and CRT   computer
                                C. computer
                                terminal

3. Match.

__ floppy disk   A. holds more infor-
__ hard disk   mation
                    B. holds less infor-
                    mation

4. Computer machines.

__ A. hardware
__ B. software

5. Match.

__ monitor   A. CRT
__ typewriter   B. keyboard

B Input and Output

Do you know what the terms *input* and *output* mean?

> **input.** The information you put into a computer.

> **output.** The information that comes out of a computer.

Question

1. Match.

__ input   **A.** use keyboard

__ output   **B.** use printer

---◆---

In the modern computer, *data entry* is normally done on a keyboard.

> **data entry.** Putting information into a computer.

Questions

1. Data entry.

__ **A.** input

__ **B.** output

2. Match.

__ data   **A.** information

__ entry   **B.** putting in

---◆---

Computers are used for *information retrieval* and *data processing.*

> **information retrieval.** Getting information out of a computer.

> **data processing.** Use of a computer to enter and organize records. When a computer figures out a customer's bill, it is doing data processing.

Questions

1. Information retrieval.

___ **A.** input

___ **B.** output

2. Match.

___ data

___ processing

A. entering and organizing

B. information

Some computers are used for **word processing.**

> **word processing.** The use of a computer to help you write memos, letters, reports, and so on. The word processing computer (**word processor**, see Chapter 2) stores what you've typed on it. You can change a letter, a word, or a line at a time. You can also give it directions to tell it how to line things up, how big the type should be, and so on. When you are all finished you can have it type out automatically the finished pages. And if you want you can have it type several copies.

Question

1. Could this book have been written on a word processing computer?

___ yes   ___ no

A computer has **memory.** A computer does what a **program** tells it to do.

> **memory.** Information stored in a computer.

> **program.** Set of directions which tells a computer how to do a particular task.

Questions

1. Computer program.

___ **A.** hardware

___ **B.** software

2. Which type of computer is likely to have a bigger memory?

___ **A.** mainframe

___ **B.** microcomputer

A computer program is written by a *computer programmer.*

computer programmer. Person skilled in one of the *computer languages* (see below) who can use this language to write up special directions to the computer.

Question

1. Computer programmer.

__ **A.** hardware specialist
__ **B.** software specialist

◆

There are many *computer languages.* Among the most common ones are *BASIC* and *COBOL.*

computer language. A special coded "language" that gives instructions to the computer. A programmer instructs the computer by using the particular language that the computer is set up to "understand."

BASIC. A fairly simple language and the most common language for microcomputers.

COBOL. A widely used language for larger computers used in business.

Questions

1. What do you use a computer language for?

__ **A.** to get it to do what you want it to do
__ **B.** to get it to talk to other computers

2. Personal computers usually use —

__ **A.** BASIC
__ **B.** COBOL

◆

Chapter Review

1. Match.

___ smallest   **A.** mainframe
___ bigger   **B.** microcomputer
___ biggest   **C.** minicomputer

2. Match.

___ keyboard   **A.** CRT
___ monitor   **B.** for data entry
___ printer   **C.** for output

3. Match.

___ hardware   **A.** machine
___ software   **B.** program

4. Match.

___ mostly a business language   **A.** BASIC
     B. COBOL
___ most common language for personal computers

5. Match.

___ computer program   **A.** to enter and organize records
___ data processing   **B.** to give instructions to computer

6. Match.

___ data entry   **A.** input
___ information retrieval   **B.** output

7. Match.

___ like a phonograph   **A.** disk drive
___ like a record   **B.** disk

8. Match.

___ for inexpensive and medium-price computers   **A.** hard disk
     B. floppy disk
___ for faster, more powerful computers

7
JOB LEGAL TERMS

Words in this chapter:

legal documents
contract
authorized signature
undersigned
witness
notary
notarized
negligence
lawsuit
liability
litigation
attorney
plaintiff
defendant
complaint
summons
served
answer

affidavit
settled out of court
trial
award of damages
judgment
lien
small claims court
arbitration
default
bankruptcy
Chapter 11
larceny
embezzlement
extortion
blackmail
fraud
forgery
vandalism

A Legal Documents and Signatures

Some of the written forms you work with on the job are likely to be *legal documents.* Before you sign one of these, be sure you understand what is says and what it means. It may be simple, but it's still probably a *contract.* And be sure you have the right to sign it and know where and how to sign it. Does it ask for an *authorized signature?* Does it talk about the *undersigned?*

legal documents. Forms which are written by lawyers and have a special meaning in a court of law.

contract. Legal agreement, particularly a legal written agreement.

authorized signature. Person who has the right to sign a particular form. You should find out on the job which kinds of forms you are authorized to sign.

undersigned. Person who signs a legal document "underneath," at the end. The language above the place for the signature will spell out what "the undersigned" is agreeing to.

Questions

1. Joshua signs a series of forms to get a loan at a loan company. Do you think these forms are legal documents?

__ yes   __ no

2. One of the forms Joshua signs says he will pay the loan company $37.88 per month. It also says what will happen if Joshua fails to make his payments. Do you think this form is a contract?

__ yes   __ no

3. Authorized.

__ **A.** allowed

__ **B.** finished

__ **C.** written

4. Undersigned.

__ **A.** line below the signature

__ **B.** person who signs the contract

__ **C.** second signature

Some legal documents ask for the signatures of **witnesses.** Some have to be **notarized.** Somebody in your office may be a **notary.** Otherwise, you can get the form notarized at a bank.

witness. A person who witnesses your signature is the person who signs right next to you to show that he or she was present when you signed.

notarized. Signed by a person who has taken a state test to enable this person to act as an official witness to a signature.

notary. Person who has the right to notarize documents. A notary has a special seal, or stamp, which can be pressed together to leave a mark on the paper with the notary's name and number. After witnessing the person's signature, the notary signs and stamps the document.

Questions

1. Here are the signatures at the bottom of a contract.

Match.

___ notary   **A.** Tom Kesel

___ undersigned   **B.** Renee Roper

___ witness (not the   **C.** Albert Smith
     notary)

2. Notary.

___ **A.** bookkeeper

___ **B.** lawyer

___ **C.** witness

3. Notarized.

___ **A.** made famous

___ **B.** no longer in effect

___ **C.** stamped and witnessed

B Lawsuits

Again, you have to be careful what you sign on the job. And you have to be careful what you do. Your *negligence* could lead to a *lawsuit.*

negligence. Carelessness that causes harm to someone.

lawsuit. Legal action in which one party sues the other, usually for money.

Questions

1. Lawsuit.

__ **A.** clothes lawyers wear

__ **B.** place where lawyers work

__ **C.** dispute that a court of law settles

2. Negligence.

__ **A.** bad intentions

__ **B.** lack of care

__ **C.** ignorance

◆

An employer has *liability* for many of the acts of its employees.

liability. Legal responsibility. An employee can make a mistake that results in legal problems that cost the employer huge amounts of money.

Question

1. If you have liability —

__ **A.** you are safe and sound

__ **B.** you may have to pay

__ **C.** you should sue

◆

Litigation is expensive. Your company doesn't want to use *attorneys* any more than it has to.

litigation. Legal action, such as a lawsuit.

attorney. Lawyer.

Questions

1. Attorney.

__ **A.** expert in business

__ **B.** expert in law

__ **C.** expert in money

2. *Litigation* means legal action. What does *to litigate* mean?

__ **A.** to go to jail

__ **B.** to judge

__ **C.** to sue

If your company does get into a lawsuit, what will it be like? First of all, there will be a *plaintiff* and a *defendant.*

plaintiff. One who sues.

defendant. The one being sued, that is, defending the lawsuit.

Question

1. The ABC Company sues the XYZ Company. Match.

__ ABC Company   **A.** defendant

__ XYZ Company   **B.** plaintiff

The plaintiff's lawyer writes up legal papers that include a *complaint* and a *summons.* The complaint and summons are usually on one legal form. They have to be *served* on the defendant. The defendant's lawyer then files an *answer.*

complaint. Says what the defendant did that was wrong and what action the plaintiff wants.

summons. Tells the defendant to appear in court to answer the complaint, in a standard, legal manner.

served. Handed to the defendant, or the representative of the defendant, in person.

answer. The defendant's side of the dispute, written up in legal form.

Questions

1. In a lawsuit, the plaintiff's papers have to be served before —

__ A. the lawsuit can continue

__ B. lawyers write up the summons

__ C. the plaintiff hires a lawyer

2. Are you usually able to serve legal papers by sending them in the mail?

__ yes   __ no

Why or why not? (In your own words.)

_____

_____

3. Match.

__ complaint   A. defendant

__ answer to complaint   B. plaintiff

4. What does a summons call for?

__ A. go to court

__ B. pay money

---◆---

The lawsuit could take a long time. While it is being prepared, the lawyers for the two sides may collect *affidavits* from people who have knowledge about important facts having to do with the case.

> **affidavit.** A written statement, signed and sworn to, about a particular fact of importance. Affidavits are widely used in law, not just in lawsuits. They can be as simple as a person swearing that he or she is the owner of a particular piece of property. They are important because they can in some circumstances be used in a court of law without the person having to show up in person.

Question

1. On an affidavit you are expected to —

__ A. keep quiet

__ B. say what sounds best

__ C. tell the truth

---◆---

74

If the lawsuit can't be *settled out of court* it will *go to trial.*

> **settled out of court.** Agreed to by the two parties on their own.

> **trial.** Legal action in a court of law.

Question

1. Match.

__ decided by a judge and jury   **A.** settled out of court

__ lawyers work out the agreement   **B.** trial

◆

At the end of the trial, the judge announces the *judgment.* If the plaintiff wins, there may be an *award of damages.* To back up the judgment, there may be a *lien* placed on the defendant's property.

> **judgment.** A legal decision at the end of a lawsuit. The judge states who wins the case — plaintiff or defendant. If the plaintiff wins, the judgment states what the defendant must do -- for example, pay money to the plaintiff.

> **award of damages.** Order by the judge for the defendant to pay money to the plaintiff. In a lawsuit, *damages* are money.

> **lien.** A legal claim on a piece of property. If the defendant doesn't pay the judgment, the plaintiff can force a sale of the property covered by the lien and get the money that way.

Question

1. As a result of a lawsuit, the Smith Co. was ordered to pay the Jones Co. $4,000. The Smith Co. finally paid. Otherwise it would have lost a building it owns.

Match.

__ damages   **A.** $4,000

__ judgment   **B.** on building

__ lien   **C.** the statement that Jones Co. won the lawsuit and that Smith Co. had to pay

◆

Some disputes can be settled in *small claims court.* Some disputes are settled by *arbitration.*

small claims court. A court set up to handle smaller claims, usually from $100 to $500. Each city sets a different limit, and in some cities the limit is as high as $1,500. Small claims court has much less red tape than a regular court.

arbitration. The settlement of a dispute by an *arbitrator* instead of by a court of law. The two sides agree to the arbitrator, who listens fairly to both sides and then makes a decision.

Questions

1. Match.

__ can do it on your own

__ usually have to hire a lawyer

A. regular lawsuit

B. sue in small claims court

2. Why do the two sides sometimes agree to arbitration, instead of going to trial?

__ **A.** costs less, less trouble

__ **B.** if they don't agree, the judge won't hear the case

__ **C.** you get bigger awards of damages

Review

1. Match.

__ notary

__ undersigned

A. official witness

B. person who signs and agrees to a contract

2. Match.

__ contract

__ lawsuit

A. legal action

B. legal agreement

3. Match.

__ liability

__ litigation

__ negligence

A. you are responsible

B. you were careless

C. you sue

4. Match.

__ affidavit

__ summons

A. has to be served

B. has to be signed and sworn to

5. Match.

__ damages

__ judgment

__ lien

A. money defendant is supposed to pay

B. states who wins a lawsuit

C. a claim on someone's property

C Common Legal Problems in Business

What happens when someone *defaults* in money it owes? To collect, the party owed money may have to go to court.

> **default.** Fail to pay.

Question

1. We sometimes say a person or company is *in default* when —

__ **A.** it collects money

__ **B.** it has paid money

__ **C.** it never paid money it owes

◆

One problem companies have is collecting money owed by another company that goes into *bankruptcy*. It may be easier if the company goes into *Chapter 11.*

> **bankruptcy.** Declaration by a court of law that a company or person is unable to pay all its debts. In most cases, the property of the bankrupt party is then split up among the people owed money.

> **Chapter 11.** Special type of bankruptcy in which the court allows a company to keep operating while giving it the right to hold off paying its debts.

Questions

1. Bankrupt.

__ **A.** broke

__ **B.** legal

__ **C.** rich

2. Chapter 11.

__ **A.** gone but not forgotten

__ **B.** six feet under

__ **C.** still hanging in there

◆

Businesses have to worry particularly about certain types of crimes. Among these are *larceny* and *embezzlement.*

larceny. Theft.

embezzlement. Special kind of theft. Embezzlement is theft by an employee of property the employee was supposed to take care of, particularly money, stocks, or bonds.

Questions

1. Embezzlement.

__ **A.** bookkeeper who steals from an employer

__ **B.** person who breaks into a house to steal

__ **C.** robber who uses a gun to hold up people

2. Larceny.

__ **A.** hurting

__ **B.** stealing

__ **C.** suing

Other crimes that businesses worry about are **extortion** (or **blackmail**), **fraud,** and **forgery.** **Vandalism** is a problem, too.

> **extortion.** Crime of getting money or property by threatening the owner.
>
> **blackmail.** Same as extortion.
>
> **fraud.** Getting something dishonestly, by trickery.
>
> **forgery.** Illegally changing a written document. Signing someone else's name to a check is forgery. So is changing a signed contract.
>
> **vandalism.** Harming or destroying property.

Questions

1. A group of criminals tell the owner of a store he will have a fire in his store if he doesn't pay them money to "protect him" against the crime.

   __ **A.** extortion
   __ **B.** fraud
   __ **C.** vandalism

2. Mary Jenkins gets hold of Sue Parker's credit card and starts using it, signing Sue Parker's name.

   __ **A.** blackmail
   __ **B.** extortion
   __ **C.** forgery

3. A group of young people break the windows of a local church.

   __ **A.** blackmail
   __ **B.** fraud
   __ **C.** vandalism

4. Alex Smith puts an ad in the paper which offers the latest record hits at very low prices. A lot of people send in money for the records. Alex takes off with the money and disappears, without ever sending the records he has promised.

   __ **A.** extortion
   __ **B.** fraud
   __ **C.** vandalism

Chapter Review

1. Match.

__ when you agree   **A.** contract

__ when you don't agree   **B.** lawsuit

2. Match.

__ carelessness   **A.** default

__ failure to pay   **B.** larceny

__ theft   **C.** negligence

3. Match.

__ before a judge   **A.** arbitration

__ the 2 sides agree to let   **B.** trial
outsider decide

4. Match.

__ by plaintiff   **A.** notarized

__ by official witness   **B.** served

__ by person who agrees   **C.** undersigned
to contract

5. Match.

__ blackmail   **A.** extortion

__ signing someone else's   **B.** forgery
name   **C.** fraud

__ use of a trick to get
someone to give you
money

6. Match.

__ bankruptcy   **A.** damaged property

__ embezzlement   **B.** stole from the boss

__ vandalism   **C.** went broke

7. Match.

__ broke but still operating   **A.** Chapter 11

__ lawsuit   **B.** litigation

__ to be served   **C.** summons

8. Match.

__ answer   **A.** by defendant

__ complaint   **B.** by plaintiff

9. Match.

__ claim on   **A.** damages
property   **B.** lien

__ money owed   **C.** judgment

__ right to collect

10. Match.

__ settled out of   **A.** agreement
court   worked out by
lawyers
__ small claims
court   **B.** you don't need a
lawyer for this

11. Match.

__ allowed   **A.** authorized

__ signed next to   **B.** witnessed
your signature

12. Match.

__ it could cost   **A.** affidavit
you money   **B.** liability

__ you swear to
the facts

13. Attorney.

__   **A.** defendant

__   **B.** judge

__   **C.** lawyer

8
CORPORATE MATTERS AND MONEY MATTERS

Words in this chapter:

incorporated
corporation
partnership
sole proprietorship
stock
share of stock
stockholder
stock certificate
public company
non-profit corporation
president
board of directors
chairman, or chairwoman, of the board
main office
corporate headquarters
branch office
department
division
lines of responsibility
assets
liabilities
net worth

receivables
payables
profitable
deficits
p and l
cash flow
equity
working capital
sales volume
revenues
financial statement
annual report
financials
audited
controller
fiscal year
calendar year
balance sheet
statement of operations
bottom line
in the red
in the black

A Corporations

Chances are that the company you work for will be *incorporated.* But not all companies are *corporations.* A great many are *partnerships* or *sole proprietorships.*

incorporated. Set up as a *corporation* (see below). To be incorporated a business has to be accepted as a corporation by the state. Each state has different rules for this. And each state has different laws and rules for how corporations are to be run.

corporation. Corporations can have many owners, although in some cases they only have one or a few owners. The owners have certain rights and duties. But they don't necessarily run the company on a day-to-day basis. On the other hand, one of the key things about a corporation is that the owners are not responsible for any debts the corporation owes. This is the major reason why many businesses incorporate.

partnership. A company that is owned by two or more people and is *not* a corporation. A partnership is simpler than a corporation. Many small businesses set up simply as partnerships. Others incorporate. And if they get large enough they almost always incorporate.

sole proprietorship. Like a partnership, a sole proprietorship is a business that is not incorporated. The difference is that a sole proprietorship is owned by only *one* person. Sole proprietorships are usually small.

Questions

1. Cynthia and Jed own the local crafts store. It is not incorporated.

   __ **A.** corporation
   __ **B.** partnership
   __ **C.** sole proprietorship

2. Fran owns the local health club — also not incorporated.

   __ **A.** corporation
   __ **B.** partnership
   __ **C.** sole proprietorship

3. Match.

   __ only one   **A.** partners
   __ two or more   **B.** sole proprietor

4. Ford Motor Co., a huge company, thousands of owners.

   __ **A.** corporation
   __ **B.** partnership
   __ **C.** sole proprietorship

Corporations issue **stock.** The stock is divided into **shares.**

> **stock.** The way corporations are owned. How much of a corporation you own depends on how many **shares** of stock you own (see below).

> **share of stock.** Each share gives you ownership of a certain part of the company.

Questions

1. **Stock,** as used here.

___ **A.** animals

___ **B.** for your feet

___ **C.** shares of a company

2. You want to buy some shares of a company. One share costs $3. How much do 100 shares cost?

$ _____

The people who own the stock of a corporation are called **stockholders** (or **shareholders**). They receive **stock certificates** for the shares they own.

> **stockholder** (or **shareholder**). Person who owns stock in a company.

> **stock certificate.** A piece of paper that legally gives a person ownership of a certain number of the corporation's shares.

Questions

1. Stockholder of a company.

___ **A.** owns a part of it

___ **B.** runs it

___ **C.** works for it

2. Stock certificate.

___ **A.** tells how big the company is

___ **B.** tells how many shares you own

___ **C.** tells how much money you made

Public companies have many stockholders.

> **public company.** A company whose stock is owned by many people, where anyone can buy or sell.

Questions

1. Public company.

___ **A.** Lorrie, her brother Charles, and her mother Sylvia are the only owners

___ **B.** IBM, a giant company with thousands of owners

2. Which is true?

___ **A.** corporations are always public companies

___ **B.** public companies are always corporations

◆

One special type of corporation is a **non-profit corporation.**

> **non-profit corporation.** Corporation set up to do such things as research or to help people in need. Non-profit corporations are not allowed to split up any profits among owners. These corporations don't have to pay most corporate taxes.

Question

1. Which is likely to be a non-profit corporation?

___ **A.** American Airlines

___ **B.** manufacturer of bubble gum

___ **C.** The Red Cross

◆

Each corporation has a **president,** a **board of directors,** and a **chairman,** or **chairwoman,** **of the board.**

> **president.** Person who runs the corporation on a day-to-day basis.

> **board of directors.** A small group of people (usually stockholders) who are expected to make important decisions about the way the corporation is to be run. The members are elected by the stockholders. They only meet once in a while. They vote on the decisions they make.

> **chairman or chairwoman (chairperson) of the board.** The person (man or woman) who is elected to run the board. The head of the board has a lot of power in the company. He or she can give orders to the president. (But in some cases, the president is also the head of the board.)

Question

1. Mr. Jones runs everything in the company — sales, marketing, billing, shipping, and so on. But he still has to take certain orders from Ms. Polanski.

   Ms. Polanski meets 3 times per year with 5 other people to make major decisions about the company. Last year they decided to hire Mr. Jones to run the company.

   Match.

   __ Mr. Jones   **A.** board of directors

   __ Ms. Polanski   **B.** chairperson

   __ Ms. Polanski   **C.** president
   and 5 others

A large corporation may have a ***main office*** with ***corporate headquarters,*** plus several ***branch offices.***

main office. The location where the most important affairs of the company are run from. The president is likely to work out of the main office.

corporate headquarters. The main office is likely to be the corporate headquarters. The finances of the company, stockholder relations, and other important corporate affairs are handled here.

branch office. A local office, not the main office. The company may have branch offices in several parts of the country. Each branch may work mainly at just one thing, usually sales.

Questions

1. The ABC Company is run from Miami. It has sales offices in Atlanta and Houston. Match.

   __ Miami   **A.** branch office

   __ Atlanta or   **B.** main office
   Houston

2. Where would you expect the corporate headquarters to be in the ABC Company (above)?

   __ **A.** Miami

   __ **B.** Atlanta or Houston

If you work for a big company you may find that it has several *departments* or *divisions.* Each department or division will have its own *lines of responsibility.*

department. Each department in a big company is responsible for a certain part of the company. For example, there may be a manufacturing department. There may be a shipping department. And there may be a sales department. There may even be different sales departments for each different product line.

division. A large part of a large company. Sometimes these large groupings are simply called departments. In other cases, they are called divisions. Each may have several subdivisions. And each subdivision may even have several departments.

lines of responsibility. As you have seen, each division or large department of a company may be responsible for several separate smaller departments. And each of these may in turn by responsible for several smaller groups. The line of responsibility runs from the head of a division or large department down to the people who run each of the separate smaller departments and then to the people who run each group. At the very top, above the heads of all the divisions, is the president of the company.

Questions

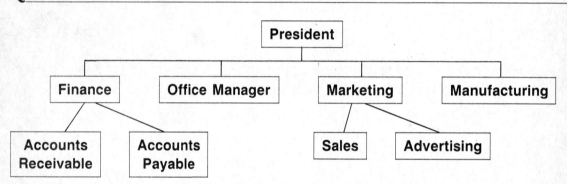

Look at the chart above. It shows the lines of responsibility in one particular company.

1. Whom does the head of the Accounts Receivable Department report directly to?

__ A. head of Finance Department
__ B. Office Manager
__ C. President

2. Whom does the Office Manager report to?

__ A. head of Finance Department
__ B. head of Marketing Department
__ C. President

3. *Division,* as used here.

__ A. in armies
__ B. in business organizations
__ C. in math problems

Review

1. Non-profit corporation.

__ **A.** had a bad year, lost money

__ **B.** helps people in need, doesn't have to pay most taxes

2. Incorporated.

__ **A.** made into a corporation

__ **B.** not a corporation

3. Match.

__ department

__ local office (like a sales office)

__ who takes orders from whom

A. branch

B. division

C. line of responsibility

4. Match.

__ owns part of company

__ runs company

__ tells how many shares

A. president

B. stockholder

C. stock certificate

5. Match.

__ a few owners, not incorporated

__ large corporation, anyone can buy and sell stock

__ only one owner

A. partnership

B. public company

C. sole proprietorship

6. Match.

__ of board of directors

__ of stock

A. share

B. chairperson

B Profit and Loss Terms

A company has **assets.** It also has **liabilities.** Subtract the one from the other and you get its **net worth.**

> **assets.** The value of everything you own. This includes your inventory, what people owe you, property you own, and so on.
>
> **liabilities.** What you owe. Your debts.
>
> **net worth.** The value of what is left over after you subtract liabilities from assets.

Questions

1. Assets $3,000,000. Liabilities $2,000,000.

   Net worth $ _____

2. Match.

   __ the copies of the new workbook we have in our warehouse   **A.** assets

   B. liabilities

   __ the money we owe the printer for the workbook

◆

Receivables are a part of assets. **Payables** are a part of liabilities.

> **receivables.** The money that customers owe you. (You've seen this word before.)
>
> **payables.** Money you owe for things you've bought.

Question

1. Match.

   __ invoices that suppliers send you   **A.** your payables

   __ invoices that you send out   **B.** your receivables

◆

Companies are not always *profitable.* Sometimes they run *deficits.*

> **profitable.** Making money.

> **deficits.** Losses.

Question

1. If you owned a company, what would you want?

__ **A.** for it to be highly profitable

__ **B.** for it to run huge deficits

People who run a company have to worry about more than the *p and l.* They also have to worry about *cash flow.*

> **p and l.** Short for **p**rofit and **l**oss. Your p and l for a particular time period is how much money you made or lost during that period.

> **cash flow.** The flow of money coming into the company and being paid out. You may need a lot of money at some periods, and not so much at others. How your cash flow works depends on when people pay you what they owe, when your bills come due, and so on. A company can be very profitable but still have problems because of cash flow.

Question

1. Money made.

__ **A.** the *p* in "p and l"

__ **B.** the *l* in "p and l"

2. Lucinda Fashions made a lot of money last year. But the company is very short on money to pay its loans.

__ **A.** profitable, but poor cash flow

__ **B.** unprofitable, but good cash flow

Even a company with a large *equity* may need extra *working capital.*

equity. Same as net worth.

working capital. Cash. Money available to do things. Not all of your assets are working capital. Part of your assets are such things as plant and equipment, which are not easily turned into cash.

Questions

1. Equity.

__ **A.** assets minus liabilities

__ **B.** liabilities minus assets

2. Working capital.

__ **A.** $100,000 worth of equipment

__ **B.** $50,000 money in the bank

__ **C.** $150,000, the sum of the 2 amounts above

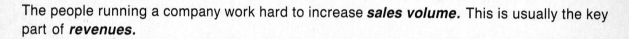

The people running a company work hard to increase *sales volume.* This is usually the key part of *revenues.*

sales volume. Amount of sales for a period.

revenues. Total income. Sales are one part of revenues. Rents you recieve are another part. So is interest on money you lend out.

Question

1. Sales volume. $300,000
   Rents. . . . . $ 20,000
   Interest . . . . $ 10,000

   Total revenues. . $_____

Review

1. Match.

__ what you owe   **A.** assets

__ what you own   **B.** liabilities

2. Match.

__ what people owe you   **A.** payables

__ what you owe people   **B.** receivables

3. Match.

__ money coming in and   **A.** cash flow
    going out

                              B. p and l

__ money you made or lost

4. Match.

__ assets minus liabilities   **A.** deficit

__ money lost   **B.** equity

5. Match.

__ ready cash   **A.** revenues

__ sales, rents, and so on   **B.** working capital

C Financial Statements

Every year, the company prepares a *financial statement.* This is presented to stockholders in an *annual report.* The *financials* are sometimes *audited* by the company's accountants.

financial statement. A complete report on what happened during a certain period in money matters, and where the company stands in terms of net worth.

annual report. Report sent out once a year to stockholders. It includes the financial statement. It may also have a message from the company president and a general report on what the company did and is planning.

financials. Short for financial statements.

audited. Checked carefully.

Questions

1. Which if these things would you expect to find in a financial statement? (Check one or more.)

__ **A.** assets

__ **B.** liabilities

__ **C.** net worth

__ **D.** profit or loss for year

__ **E.** revenues for year

2. Why are financials sometimes audited?

__ **A.** to correct the numbers

__ **B.** to correct the spelling

__ **C.** to correct the shares

3. Our last annual report covered the period ending October 31 last year. Our next annual report will cover the period ending —

__ **A.** November 31

__ **B.** December 31

__ **C.** October 31 this year

A large company will have a **controller.** The controller manages the bookkeepers and may be responsible for such things as receivables and payables. The controller is also responsible for financial statements.

> **controller.** Person in charge of the financial area of a company. Sometimes spelled *comptroller,* but still pronounced "controller."

Question

1. Controller.

__ **A.** marketing person
__ **B.** money person
__ **C.** salesperson

A company's *fiscal year* doesn't have to be the same as the *calendar year.*

> **fiscal year.** The yearly period the company sets for figuring out its yearly financial statement. The fiscal year can begin on any day. It usually depends on the day the company was incorporated. Educational Design's fiscal year begins November 1 and ends October 31.

> **calendar year.** The regular year. It begins January 1 and ends December 31.

Questions

1. New Year's Day is the first day of —

__ **A.** the calendar year
__ **B.** Educational Design's fiscal year

2. Some companies have the same fiscal year as the calendar year. When does their fiscal year end?

_____

The financials wil include a *balance sheet* and a *statement of operations.* It's the statement of operations that tells you the *bottom line.* It will tell you whether you're *in the red* or *in the black.*

> **balance sheet.** The part of the financials that tells you your assets, liabilities, and net worth on a specific date.

> **statement of operations.** The part of the financials that tells you what happened during the year in money terms — what your revenues were, how much you spent, and so on. At the end it tells you how much money you made or lost.

> **bottom line.** The amount at the bottom of the operations summary, the number that tells you how much money you made or lost — after all the addition or subtraction.

> **in the red.** Losing money.

> **in the black.** Profitable. Bookkeepers sometimes use red ink to show a loss and black ink to show a profit.

Questions

1. A company going broke.

__ **A.** in black

__ **B.** in red

2. Match.

__ in black   **A.** controller happy

__ in red   **B.** controller sad

3. Your bottom line tells you —

__ **A.** your p and l

__ **B.** your receivables

__ **C.** your revenues

4. Match.

__ balance sheet   **A.** net worth

__ statement of operations   **B.** p and l

94

Chapter Review

1. Match.

__ has board of directors

__ not incorporated, several owners

__ only one owner

A. corporation

B. partnership

C. sole proprietorship

2. Match.

__ elected by board of directors

__ runs company on day-to-day basis

A. chairperson

B. president

3. Match.

__ helps people in need

__ lost money

A. deficit

B. non-profit company

4. Match.

__ in balance sheet

__ in statement of operations

A. equity

B. revenues

5. Match.

__ money you owe

__ plant, equipment, receivables, and so on

__ subtract one from the other

A. assets

B. liabilities

C. net worth

6. Match.

__ each company has its own

__ regular year

A. calendar year

B. fiscal year

7. Match.

__ checked

__ had a deficit

__ profitable

A. audited

B. in the black

C. in the red

8. Match.

__ probably has corporate headquarters

__ local office

A. branch office

B. main office

9. Match.

__ money in and out

__ ready cash

A. cash flow

B. working capital

10. Match.

__ p and l

__ stock

A. bottom line

B. share

11. Match.

__ owns part of company

__ works for company

A. controller

B. stockholder

12. Match.

__ big departments

__ who reports to whom

A. divisions

B. lines of responsibility

13. Match.

__ part of revenues

__ part of working capital

A. money in bank

B. sales volume

14. Match.

__ part of annual report

__ stock in company

A. financials

B. shares